I0458132

## Accolades for Debby's Writing

"Keep being more of you."

Willie Taylor

"I love the way you write.

Dana Mahoney

"Such a great writer! Keep up the good work!"

Deborah McDonald

"You have made quite an impact on a lot of people."

Coach Wayne Miller

# Soul Stories

**Poetry From
the Heart**

Debby Hackbarth

Debby Hackbarth

Copyright © 2025 Debby Hackbarth


ISBN: 978-1-961485-97-6 Paperback
ISBN: 978-1-961485-98-3 Hardback


FV 4


Without limiting the rights under copyright reserved above, no part
of this publication may be reproduced, stored in or introduced into a
retrieval system, or transmitted, in any form, or by any means
(electronic, mechanical, photocopying, recording, or otherwise),
without the prior written permission both of the copyright owner
and the above listed publisher of this book.


The scanning, uploading, and distribution of this book via the
Internet or via any other means without the permission of the
publisher is illegal and punishable by law. Please purchase only
authorized electronic editions, and do not participate in or
encourage electronic piracy of copyrighted material. Your support of
the author's rights is appreciated.

Published by:

Intellect Publishing, LLC

www.IntellectPublishing.com

# Dedication

This collection of poetry is dedicated to the following:

My Heavenly Father, who formed me in my mother's womb to have a nature of servant leadership.

My husband, who has lovingly stood by my side for over fifty years. He is my rock.

My publisher, who continues to amaze me with his talents and compassionate nature.

My children and grandchildren, who fill my life with joy.

My friends, who continue to inspire me daily.

Debby Hackbarth

# Author's Note and Acknowledgements

Although my first composition was a skit for my third-grade classroom, my first love has always been poetry. Before college, I focused my creative energy into the theater. During college, I continued being involved in theater and started writing poetry.

In retirement, my supportive husband helped me start my business, HAART, LLC, which promotes my writing. He has taken over so many of our responsibilities, so that I may write. In addition, I met Coach Miller and John Woods, who paved the way for my work to be published.

Several writing groups continue to encourage my writing journey: Pensters Writing Group, The Writer's Club, Inner Circle Writers' Group, Alabama Writers Cooperative, and Alabama State Poetry Society.

Thank you to all of these wonderful lovers of the written word.

Debby Hackbarth

# Table of Contents

Dedication p. iii

Author's Note and Acknowledgments p. v

## Chapter One: Animals

A New Pet p. 4

Considerate Conduct p. 5

Uncommon Canine p. 6

Bovines p. 8

Cat Control p. 9

Feline Focus p. 11

Magnificent Mammals p. 12

Camelopard Craving p. 13

## Chapter Two: Family

Spurred to Succeed p. 16

A Beaded Pair p. 18

Grandma Ruby p. 19

Grandma Lucille p. 20

In the Blood p. 21

Loving Words p. 22

Absent Hero p. 23

| | |
|---|---|
| Devotion | p. 24 |
| Butterscotch Blunder | p. 26 |
| The Red Truck | p. 27 |
| Midwest Childhood | p. 29 |
| Friendship Can Foster Fate | p. 31 |
| Young Love | p. 32 |
| Newlyweds | p. 34 |
| Committed Champion | p. 35 |
| Motherhood | p. 36 |
| Busted and Broken | p. 37 |
| Fifty Years Together | p. 38 |

## Chapter Three: Friends

| | |
|---|---|
| Extreme Survival | p. 42 |
| Frightful Find | p. 43 |
| Enchanting Twilight | p. 45 |
| Mysterious Meandering | p. 46 |
| Forever Friends | p. 48 |
| Rescue, Recovery, Renewal | p. 50 |
| Unyielding and Unbroken | p. 51 |
| Celebrations | p. 52 |

Ridicule                           p. 53

## Chapter Four: Inspiration

Respond to the Outcry             p. 56

Inspire, Initiate, Ignite          p. 57

Butterfly Transformation           p. 58

Never Underestimate                p. 59

Humorous or Hurtful                p. 60

Leave A Mark                       p. 61

Do What's Right                    p. 63

Perseverance                       p. 65

Little Towhead                     p. 67

Spreading Encouragement            p. 69

Transformation                     p. 70

## Chapter Five: Nature

Outside                            p. 73

Pursuing Peace                     p. 75

Rolling Waves                      p. 76

The Ocean, A Forever Friend        p. 78

Searching and Soaring              p. 79

The Dream                          p. 81

Incorporate Kindness                          p. 82

Miss Jane on the Train                        p. 83

## Chapter Six: Society

Return To Compassion                          p. 87

Butterflies Into Bliss                        p. 89

Failing Fatherhood                            p. 90

Stand Up for Yourself                         p. 91

Enduring Exploration                          p. 92

Living In Unity                               p. 93

Marvelous Multiplicity                        p. 94

Value Others                                  p. 95

Parenting: Not An Easy Task                   p. 97

We Need Redemption                            p. 98

Significant                                   p. 99

Darkness, Disaster, Dream                     p. 100

Sparkle In Every Situation                    p. 101

Unrestrained Rule                             p. 103

Afterword                                     p. 105

# Soul Stories

## Poetry From
## the Heart

Debby Hackbarth

# Chapter One: Animals

Humans prosper when animals are in their lives. Our lives are deeply enriched by being in close proximity to any creature.

Wherever you live, make sure you can enjoy the presence of God's creatures.

Debby Hackbarth

## A New Pet

My search has just begun.
He loves them all, you see.
My quest is for my son.
To fill his life with glee.

I think he wants a dog.
Maybe a silky cat.
Can't seem to find a frog.
Should I look for a bat?

I need to hurry now.
The store's about to close.
I made a solemn vow.
Hope he likes what I chose.

## **Considerate Conduct**

Encouragement can emanate from any living entity.

Reassurance and unconditional love come from considerate conduct.

Mom told me that "best things come in small packages".

Pets are the most precious and petite parcels.

Most of my life, canines were my constant companions.


I was taught to provide considerate and committed care.

When mom fell on tough times, our dogs suffered.

She could only afford to feed them and love them.

I promised myself I would provide a great life for a rescue.

Three beauties blessed our lives over many years.

Debby Hackbarth

## Uncommon Canine

Timid, Nervous, Fearful
She was anxious and bashful.
We were thrilled to adopt her.
She was pretty and demure.

Farrah filled our lives with joy.
Love puppy, her only toy.
She slept in her giant crate.
Outside our room, no debate.

Stupid of me to not crate her.
"It's only a few minutes, sir."
Mild-mannered momma taught us.
Her fear of desertion rocked us.

Thoughtless, Foolish, Reckless,
Appropriate words, I confess.
The minutes we left her alone.
Teachable moment, milestone.

Our calm lady became forceful.
Door opening was masterful.
Interior doors were ajar.
Luckily, she did not get far.

That was so stupid of me.
Now we're a family of three.
She needed to feel secure.
Many months of love, the cure.

Debby Hackbarth

## Bovines

I constantly hear a cat's meow.

I'd rather spend my time with a cow.

Into my life, a bovine I'll allow.

Since I'm a city dweller, I don't know how.


I've got to find a way, somehow.

Let's chat; have a powwow.

I don't care if others raise an eyebrow.

I'd like one, here and now.

## **Cat Control**

Have you ever had an elegant Sphynx strut
past you?

Did a gorgeous tabby tug on your heartstrings?

Were you smitten with a dark-faced Siamese?


Folks want a cat to dominate their domiciles.

Think again when you adopt a fabulous feline.

The human is no longer in control of his/her
existence.


Charlie Chartreux or Buddy Birman are the
kings now.

What can one do to survive in this new
situation?

Will other kitty owners help rescue your sanity?


The best advice is to give them unconditional
love.

Continuous cat control is not the end of
actuality.

Find new ways to enjoy life when you are not
the boss.

Debby Hackbarth

Cuddle up with your Maine Coon on winter
nights.

Chase your American Bobtail around the
house.

Show off your elegant Bombay Cat on
Halloween.


Will there be cats in the afterlife?

Will they be waiting to love us?

Will they be curious to connect with us?

Will they be eager to exhibit their
exquisiteness?


Their kindness and compassion kiss my
countenance.

Their graceful gait gloriously winds around me.

Command me to constantly show them
compassion.

Please permit my life to be filled with felines.

## **Feline Focus**

A brown dog, A black cat, A green frog, A white rat.

A pet is my top priority but, I don't want them all.

Giant or small in size; a cat would really please me.


A black kitten, my first choice, followed by a bright-eyed tabby.

I want to buy one today, but I can't find a marvelous match.

I don't have enough money to pay for a perfect pet.


I'll come back another day to acquire a magnificent mouser.

My goal is to focus on funds to finance a fine feline.

I desperately desire a companion for cozy comfort.

Next month, a new cat will rule my humble residence.

Debby Hackbarth

## Magnificent Mammals

I want to behold,

Their brilliant beauty,

Fluff freckled with light and color.

Fabulous felines, God's gift to us.


They stride in deafening silence.

They thrive in terrifying tranquility.

They attack in surprising seconds.

Surround me with your splendid self-
importance.


The sensation of their fur upon my skin,

Causes me to calmy contemplate,

How a creator crafted their corporal shells.

How could such a miracle materialize?


The first feline, fantastically fashioned,

Majestically made for mankind.

Autonomous, unattached, exceptional.

## Camelopard Craving

When wonder began, I don't recall.
Did I see them on television?
Take me to a zoo not a shopping mall.
Can we leave without conversation?

I long to be close to them, so tall.
Will I die from anticipation?
Giraffes graceful gait does enthrall.
How could there be such perfection?

I'll always love them; I'm an oddball.
Can we go there on vacation?
I view them from behind a wall.
Aren't they God's special creation?

Debby Hackbarth

# Chapter Two: Family

Every family has its secrets and stories. My family features fabulous females from multiple generations: authors, artists, dancers, mentors, hikers, and volunteers.

However, we could not have been as successful without our supportive spouses, outstanding offspring, and glorious grandchildren.

Debby Hackbarth

## Spurred to Succeed

I spent hours researching family tales.

I hoped to find regal Celtic females.

Getting nowhere, I felt downright downcast.

Suddenly, an Irish woman spoke; I was
aghast!


A gateway made our chat comprehensible.

Her delightful words were incomparable.

Queen Shioban shared she was staunch, but
little

Like her, I was tiny; never second-fiddle.


We spoke at length, sharing our lives of pain.

Both of us walked paths that seemed insane.

Each day brought another ugly insult.

Ruling in a world of males was definitely
difficult.


Equestrians both, we loved to ride.

Being on horseback healed wounds inside.

Her loving encouragement caused my fear to flee.

In her honor, powerful people bent the knee.

Shioban governed with compassionate insight.

She was a fervent female who did what's right.

Never let distress or dread damage your reign.

Never lead with anger; from rage abstain.

She overcame the impossible to powerfully lead.

Her determination and wisdom spurred me to succeed.

Debby Hackbarth

## A Beaded Pair

Found it by mistake.
Took a double-take.
Smaller than an I-pad.
Older than my granddad.
Beaded and sparkling,
Dressy and dazzling.
Use if when you go out.
Really, it's a knockout.
Colors I would pick.
Lovely, fantastic.
Hues of blue, beige, and gold.
Can't believe it's that old.
Framed, look through the glass.
Yes, it is first class.
The body so ornate.
The clasp does operate.
No, you can't have it.
I bet the dress would fit.
A flapper dress and bag, so grand.
Something out of fantasyland.

## Grandma Ruby

Ruby made art from broken glass.
She gave us socks that glistened.
Dirty dishes would rarely pass.
But to her stories we listened.

Her home in Chicago was quite small.
Three rooms on each floor and a basement.
The five of us didn't mind at all.
We wished our visits were more frequent.

One bathroom on the second floor.
We had to go upstairs alone.
"Don't open any other door."
This rule forced us to groan.

Bathroom journey, I was resolute.
I peered into her closet.
Shockingly, it was full of loot.
Tons of toilet paper, a safety net.

Debby Hackbarth

## Grandma Lucille

Lucille was a gentle soul.

Her laugh would fill a room.

Through her neighborhood we would stroll.

Smelling her sweet perfume.


She lived in a tiny space.

An apartment filled with smiles.

Freedom to explore her place.

It seemed to go on for miles.


One day I decided to explore.

Enchanted by her attire.

Old clothes in her closet quite a bore.

Her jewelry I came to admire.


Lu wore lipstick every day.

Clip-on earrings to match her dress.

Blueberry pancakes on Sunday.

She favored me to excess.

## In the Blood

During the Great War, granddad was a Marine.
In WW II, dad's minesweeper led the way.
Irish and English heritage is in every gene.
Let me relax and revive in the sand on the bay.

Raised in the corn fields of the Midwest.
My dream was to visit the salty sea.
How could I ever accomplish this quest?
A seafaring lass was what I wanted to be.

Over time, my life became more aquatic.
I swam for hours and was nicknamed Fish.
But I longed to be oceanic.
How could I possibly fulfill this wish?

In my teens, my family went to Cape Cod.
The smell and sounds of the ocean filled me.
It seemed like an awesome act of God.
My seagoing blood was finally free.

Debby Hackbarth

## Loving Words

Mom's loving words were unsurpassed.

She assured me; I was downcast.

Peace was not near, just tumult.

Doubt and fear were the result.


Mom shared how she was harassed.

Lu felt outside the mold, outcast.

She told me her life was difficult.

Each day brought an insult.


She overcame and learned to lead.

Her promptings pushed me to succeed.

When I wasn't able to see; Lu found the best
care.

Sacrificial love using money they couldn't
spare.


Amazingly, my parents were partners in crime.

They worked overtime to help me to climb.

I cherished our hours of sharing tales.

Now I fathom we're both fierce females.

## Absent Hero

Dad was continually working.

However, he never stopped caring.

When I was born, he stopped playing.

Football was replaced with his offspring.


Through the years, he was a sales king.

For our survival, income he'd bring.

Silver dollars from him sure did bling.

Still, we lived on a tiny shoestring.


We all wished we could do something.

As time passed; work was still everything.

To see him more we'd give anything.

Now he's gone and it really does sting.

Debby Hackbarth

## Devotion

I was born five weeks premature.
Toxins from mom I could not endure.

Daily mother's milk was supplied.
Teeny Dee was ready to thrive.

I heard the story about a mustard seed.
Mom cited the proverb to help me to lead.

A tiny bit of faith can do the impossible.
This ongoing chat made my survival plausible.

When I couldn't breathe, for hours I'd yelp.
When I couldn't see, I would call for help.

Lu repeated the story to calm me.
Her unwavering love caused fear to flee.

I still call to her even though she's passed.

Her words still cause me to remain steadfast.

Lu created a tornado, full of strength.

To aid my offspring, I'll go to any length.

Debby Hackbarth

## Butterscotch Blunder

Her butterscotch dessert was always a treat.
However, this time it looked like grey concrete.
Did she use an unusually high heat?
When I tasted it, my face was as red as a beet.
The flavor was awful like the smell of dirty
feet.
How could I quickly flee and retreat?


My mother's stare I didn't want to greet.
I covered my mouth and ran to the street.
How could golden pudding turn to cement?
I could not show her my discontent.
Mom ran after me with well intent.
Could she really correct my dissent?


I really wanted to give her a complement.
She certainly viewed my agonizing torment.
"Mom, can we please discuss this even?"
Our loving conversation was time well spent.
Turned out it was a bad experiment.

## The Red Truck

My dolls were always in full view.

Playing with them was not taboo.

Bring my truck outside, I'd not dare.

I found a space to get away.

My attic room, a place to play.

No one could bully me there.


Tiny girl, enormous truck.

How could I have all the luck?

My taste surely rocked the boat.

This splendid truck was cherry red.

I hid my prize under my bed.

I loved its shiny metal coat.


I longed to be a fireman.

The red truck ignited my plan.

I shared my dream with my best friend.

The pals did quench many a fire.

To save the dolls we would conspire.

We wished our quests would never end.

I moved across town when I was ten.

I searched for Red like a mother hen.

I refused to believe he was gone.

Who would hide my beloved red toy?

Who'd be mean enough to take my joy?

I was miserable and withdrawn.


Daily I would beseech and plea.

My parents never answered me.

Soon I swapped pain with happiness.

New puppies in the house made me glad.

I could move away from being mad.

A different focus brought cheerfulness.

## **Midwest Childhood**

Lombard is the Lilac Town.
A famous spot of renown.

We lived in a tiny Cape Cod.
To the five of us, it wasn't odd.

Two girls, one boy shared one room.
We were siblings of the baby boom.

One bathroom for five wasn't too bad.
Having our own backyard made us glad.

School came at the age of four.
Bullying made the fun, a chore.

No one wore glasses in my class.
Hearing "4 eyes" was just too crass.

Dad's accident gave us money.
This made Mom's life very sunny.

Debby Hackbarth


A brick house in a fancy locale.
PTA president, quite the gal.


No air strip here but miles to hike.
We shouted, "what's not to like?


As time went on, we lost the house.
Mom was unhappy with her spouse.


High school was bursting with good times.
Honors classes, theater lines.


Tiny Debby, ready for college.
Leaving home, acquiring knowledge.

**Friendship Can Foster Fate**


Common comrades care.

Bob worked with both of us.

Bob set up the rendezvous.


A movie, a meal, polite discourse.

Should I give love a chance?

He was handsome.

He was polite.


Springtime in Fairhope, breathtaking.

Milky-white dogwood petals float ubiquitously.

A season of warmth.

A season of joy.



We've hiked for years along the bay.

A time for affection.

A time for meditation.

Debby Hackbarth

## Young Love

It's strange to be analyzing another regarding
his life and yours.

When someone occurs in my life, why should I
constantly play a game of pro and con?

I enjoy being with him is that not enough?

I do not wish to change his personality or soul.


I constantly think about him: events and
thoughful things he does.

His handsome face and "bod".

How he could enhance his own good looks?

Of course thoughts about sex enter in.

Will he still care when he knows I am old-
fashioned?

I've heard some sex is fine, but too much ruins
a relationship.


What does he like: modern décor,
Mediterranean, contemporary?

I know (like me) that he enjoys: plays, dinner
out, running, nature, poetry, calm music, rock
(once in a while), non-violence, ice cream,
movies, spiritual.

# Soul Stories

But, does he like: ballet, dancing, yogurt (I
think so), waffles, rainbows, horseback riding?

Does he feel children should have a good
religious background?

I know he enjoys prayer, but would he like my
church?


So many questions. Does he have any? I'm
sure he does.

You're strong and gentle; quiet and loud;
complimenting and criticizing; gay and serious.

Because you are a man.

Your appearance is "straight", but your mind is
"semi".

Who knows what the future will hold.


Will we "get together"; decide it's just or fun;
split up?

I will trust in God and know He will do the best
for both of us.

Whatever happens, Jim, you are a unique
individual and I do care.

Let's let time be our teacher and God be our
guide.

Debby Hackbarth

## Newlyweds


With you, I feel complete and content.

Without you, I feel alone and alienated.

These past four months have been heavenly to
me. You are the best think that has happened
in my life.


I know that our life will be full of wonderful
events and growth will be mutual and
profitable for both of us.

Sometimes I am very trying.

Sometimes I do not bring you joy.

Sometimes I do not enjoy all that I should.
FORGIVE ME.


I thank you for helping me mentally, physically,
and spiritually.

I do hope that I have done the same for you.

I do so want to make you happy and content.


No matter what anyone else says, does, thinks,
sees, or feels: I LOVE YOU.

Happy Anniversary Dearest One.

## Committed Champion

Most folks would love to have a secret
guardian.

A companion to serve as a committed
champion.

A partner who is more than a personal
protector.

A friend facing conflicts like a fearless fighter.

I've had several comrades who've been my
heroes.

In fact, life was so challenging they seemed
like superheroes.

Every person never acted like a cautious
caretaker.

Instead, each one safeguarded me like a
crusader.

Many years have gone by and my mate is my
shield.

In his arms I find sensitive and sympathetic
shelter.

My desire is that you find someone to be by
your side.

With your comrade close to you, you'll never
need to hide.

Debby Hackbarth

## Motherhood

Some say it's merely a guardianship.
Others announce it's a joyful journey.
A few reveal it's a difficult duty.
What does motherhood signify to me?

For a time, it seemed innocently inaccessible.
Difficult days, it was deemed improbable.
I didn't know a stupendous son was forming.
After long hours, a beautiful boy arrived.

Motherhood made a marvelous milestone.
Human words cannot convey the limitless love.
Recovery was arduous and drawn-out.
Should I try again for more offspring?

The path overshadowed pain and poverty.
Two lovely ladies entered our modest domicile.
Unconditional adoration was overwhelming.
Motherhood develops a devotion that's eternal.

## Busted and Broken

Solitude, silence, chaos, and confusion,
My troubled mind fluctuated.
Fear stoked the thumping and thrashing.
My brain seemed busted and broken.


A concept was clouting.
Can I traverse the terror?
I decided to deeply delve.
Peeking into private places.


My dread was being deserted.
Shut away in a tiny room; alone and forgotten.
I reached out to my best friend.
Could he help me resolve this?


He hurried to my room to help
Sharing until my shivers were sacked.
Now my anxiety was exposed.
We vowed to never be apart.

Debby Hackbarth

## Fifty Years Together

The old saying is that "opposites attract".
If you saw us, you'd say that's true.


He's tall; it looks like my height was hijacked.
My eyes are bluish-gray and his are soft blue.


Athletics was his passion; I preferred a theater
act.
Due to distance and devotions, our dating hit a
snafu.


The picture he kept in his locker made an
impact.
I moved on, but he had a different point of
view.


When college ended, our new lives were jam-
packed.
But through it all, he loved me through and
through.


This big, strong man's tenderness was indeed
a class act.

I couldn't believe that little me would finally
say "I do".

Over fifty years together and we've never been
side-tracked.

The tiny thespian and the talented track star
remain true.

Debby Hackbarth

## Chapter Three: Friends

"A good friend is like a four-leaf clover; hard to find and lucky to have." —Irish Proverb

Those of us who've had good friends through the years know how valuable they are in our lives.

I've had several loving friends who were and continue to be closer to me than some of my relatives.

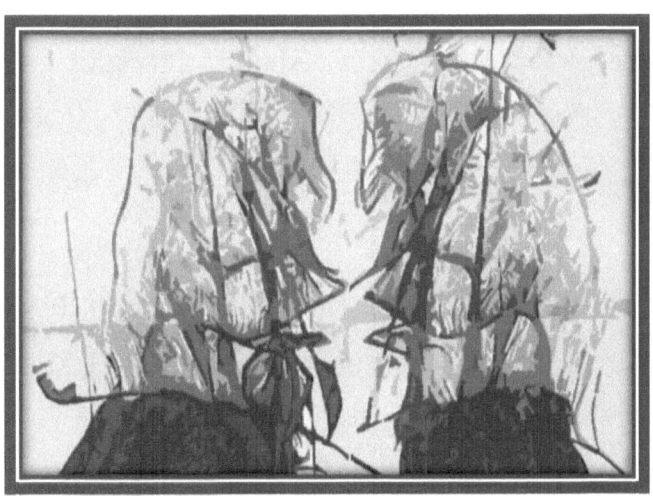

Debby Hackbarth

## Extreme Survival

My friends and I play online every day.
We go on adventures, come what may.
Worlds to explore throughout the universe.
Creatures and challenges quite diverse.
Monsters, military, foes, and friends.
These planets consume us, until we end.
Next time our quests continue unsurpassed.
We face combat with weapons at full blast.

Our teams battle feverishly to win.
We're frantic when in a tailspin.
But we don't give up; we're pals, you see.
Helping each other, brave and free.
Success in the fantasy domains.
Gives us confidence; strengthens our brains.
We'll be leaders wherever we go.
Skills and strength the world to show.

## Frightful Find

"How did they get there?"

All we could do was stare.


"Was this someone's secret lair?"

The placement took great care.


"Jack, can you move the masonry square?"

All Rosy could do was observe and glare.


"I need muscles, Sam, can you put your hand
there?"

Sam skipped toward Jack, with his usual flair.


Lucy commented: "This whole scene is quite
rare!"

It looked like something out of a nightmare.


Rosy said: "Yikes, the couple's clothes look
threadbare!"

Such a mystery because gold jewelry was
everywhere.

Sam said: "Let's leave everything alone and find the heir."

Jack took pictures so the bones he'd not impair.


"Should we cover them gently so others won't have a scare?"

The four friends concealed the site gently with little fanfare.

## **Enchanting Twilight**

The moon was absent this enchanting twilight.
We were wrapped in a dark, moonless night.
The fog filled us with flummoxing fright.
Walking home in terror was our perilous plight.

Darkness choked us making our throats tight.
Even the stars were blocked from our eyesight.
What did we do to deserve this ghastly blight?
Why couldn't Joe bring his favorite flashlight?

Sally spied a dimly lit cabin, to our delight.
Her words hit us like a massive meteorite.
We had hope everything would be all right.
All five of us ran to the hut with all our might.

Often, we get our best ideas in hindsight.
This ill-planned journey provided insight.
Consider intuitions, no matter how slight.
Plan out your quests early, at first light.

Debby Hackbarth

## Mysterious Meandering

We were an adventurous trio: two girls and a
boy.

Our weekly treks throughout the woods
generated joy.


One autumn hike brought cool weather and
downed branches.

We constantly cut the boughs to improve our
hiking chances.


Our frequent journeys were meant to explore,
not destroy.

But this day we altered mother nature, a
voyage to enjoy.


On this unfamiliar path, we were filled with
intense delight.

Sam suggested that we keep going until we
need a flashlight.


Shortly, our mysterious meandering suffered a
new turn.

The flashlight failed in the darkening forest; a
cause for concern.

# Soul Stories

Did the woodland want to punish us for doing
her harm?

Could we ever find out way home to the family
farm?


This mystery worried us, but we needed to
make a plan.

Suzie decided to climb a nearby tree, the
region to scan.


Turns out we were going in circles and were
close to home.

Sam soon spied our neighbor's yurt, fashioned
like a dome.


We trudged on toward our barn, ready to
devour refreshments then rest.

Our wonderful wandering produced willpower
to overcome another test.

Debby Hackbarth

**Forever Friends**

Melding with nature is marvelous.
Being there with friends, so fabulous.
Everyone planned using common sense.
Looking for times that weren't intense.

Traveling through terrific terrain.
We disregarded insects and rain.
Nothing would stop us.
A terrific trio, a plus.

Overlooking the weather, we went.
Snubbing the time, we were not spent.
We brought lots of snacks to eat.
To suit us all, they were salty and sweet.

In younger days, we vanished for hours.
Our plastic hoodies held off rain showers.
Often, we huddled together.
We could endure soggy weather.

# Soul Stories

Finally, one day we did get lost.
Three different signals got crisscrossed.
Should we ask for help?
Could we scream and yelp?

We agreed to back track to the start.
We knew, to keep safe, don't be apart.
What plants did we see?
Which structures were key?

We found our path; we were home free.
No one shared the spine-tingling spree.
We had new skills for our trips.
Now equipped for hardships.

Older now, we continue to walk.
Enjoying nature, a time to talk.
Forever friends to the end.
Time together we'll always spend.

Debby Hackbarth

**Rescue, Recovery, Renewal**

Some view redemption as a renewal of a
friendship.

Others see the same term as deliverance from
a tough situation.

Whatever way you look at the word, it involves
perseverance.

I didn't know if I had the strength to make it
work.

For years, we had a loving and empathetic
fellowship.

Challenging careers had put us in a daunting
position.

Hours and miles apart hindered a continuance.

Our bond needed a revitalization if we were to
succeed.

Fortunately, a close friend rescued our
relationship.

She created a new company with unbelievable
determination.

After reaching out to us, she presented an
alliance.

Emancipation and recovery thanks to a caring
colleague.

Soul Stories

## **Unyielding and Unbroken**

A dependable person is like a firm foundation.
A friend who keeps you in a secure position.

Concrete is composed of sand and water.
Over time, a crumbling does indeed matter.

A genuine relationship is strong and steadfast.
A trustworthy team is undeniably quantifiable.

Find comrades who are consistently
compassionate.

True pals are not rigid, but are your stable
safety net.

Seek companions whose devotion is unyielding
and unbroken.

Debby Hackbarth

## Celebrations

Sunshine complemented their smiles.

Gentle breezes kissed her white dress.

Family sent love across the miles.


The beautiful couple exchanged their vows.

Tears of joy were shed in many places.

This precious union was long awaited.


Magnificent flowers did not need vases.

The island setting augmented their love.

This spring has been a time to dance.


Summer will see many celebrations.

A long life together is not by chance.

God had them in His hand from the onset.

## Ridicule

We were taught the "Golden Rule"
Don't harass and ridicule.
Always think of others first,
Do the best and not the worst.

Every time we tried to play,
It could only be her way.
I was kind and she was not,
Always lesser, tiny spot.

Day by day I tried my best.
She caused me to be stressed.
She loved to assume command,
Insult, bully, and cajole. Often it got out of
hand.

To cope with it all, I became numb.
But I am certainly not dumb.
I hope help comes down her lane,
A relationship, I'll refrain.

Debby Hackbarth

## Chapter Four: Inspiration

We are not on this Earth to be alone, without relationships. When we run to escape hurt and pain into a dark place alone; often we spiral downward.

We need each other.

Ever since I was a child, I have sought to reach out and help others. It has not always been easy; however, I'm so happy when another person's spirits have been lifted.

Debby Hackbarth

## Respond to the Outcry

For as long as I can remember, I wanted to fly.

Not in an airplane, but like a superhero.

I would fly facedown like a beautiful butterfly.

Floating above the power lines so I wouldn't
glow.

I'd glide gracefully like a delightful dragonfly.

People might ponder; is she friend or foe?

Coasting along the air currents as they
intensify.

No one would be frightened of my spectacular
show.

If someone was in trouble, I'd respond to the
outcry.

I would not hesitate; I'd just get up-and-go.

But like other humans, this talent did not
apply.

However, I could still help others to prosper
and grow.

I can be a daily superhero who's not in the
public eye.

## Inspire, Initiate, Ignite

"I want to play football."
"No, you can be a mom."

"I want to be a fireman."
"No, wear a pretty dress to prom."

I wanted desperately to reveal,
That I could leave a mark.

I'd seen both genders perform well.
I wanted to ignite a spark.

I chose to inspire others by action and pen.
So, I decided to tell tales and teach.

Slowly at first, but then a powerhouse.
Many hundreds of folks I was able to reach.
Don't settle for others' expectations.

Debby Hackbarth

## Butterfly Transformation

Growing up, I always wanted to fly.
As a child, I even gave it a try.
Watching the butterflies by the hour.
I would flap my arms, hoping to soar.
Their beauty was an inspiration.
My humanity was an inhibition.
As a teen, I learned that butterflies were free.
My turbulent family was crashing around me.

I wanted to ride with the monarchs.
I wanted to salute the red admirals.
Dare I become a painted lady?
Should I strut like the peacock butterfly?
Butterflies are symbols of joy and hope.
There was no time to sit and mope.
As I aged, my life transformed.
Like a butterfly, I was reborn.

## Never Underestimate

Came five weeks early, created to survive,
Tiny like a mustard seed, ready to thrive.
Oxygen bolstered her lungs of little size,
Survival was more important than her eyes.


ENDURANCE, PERSISTENCE, ETERMINATION.


Mother's milk strengthened her in the hospital,
Love toughened her to never be second fiddle.
Born from a long line of fabulous females,
Leaders across decades, always blazing trails.


DANCERS, POETS, ARTISANS, TRAILBLAZERS


Weeks of nurses and months of restless nights,
Persevered through colic, boy did she fight!
This strenuous start sparked her stalwart self,
A tiny tornado, sure of herself.


BEWARE, NEVER UNDERESTIMATE.

Debby Hackbarth

## Humorous or Hurtful

When you're unique, folks can be hurtful.
Their actions and words can be cruel.
How could they possibly be thoughtful?
Don't they understand you're a jewel?

I'm choosing not to be sorrowful.
I will follow the tough path of renewal.
Finding humor in life can help you to shine.
No longer will my life be in decline.

I will use wit and laughter to sparkle.
My crossed eyes will start to twinkle.
No longer will my candle be a faint light.
I will replace hurt with joy and constantly fight.

Wounding words will no longer harm me.
May I encourage others to also be free.

## Leave A Mark

Fighting the Iroquois Fire in Chicago.

Saving dwellings in Melrose Park.

Many men in my family were firemen.

Every time an engine went by, I was aglow.

The flashy red trucks left an indelible mark.

I asked for my own truck again and again.

For Christmas, I got the truck from the TV
show.

My parents' gift hit it out of the ballpark.

I protected my prize like a mother hen.

When my prized possession was lost, I turned
to the piano.

Two years on the piano and my world went
dark.

"We need the money to pay bills – no piano
then."

Debby Hackbarth


"Girls cannot be fire fighters." What a blow!

"Ok then, I'll play football in a ballpark."

"Girls can't play football, dear Adrienne."


"If I could have, I would have" became my tale of woe.

But I was desperate to disclose I could leave a mark.

I'd seen women outperform men, now and then.


A fireman or a football player – not the status quo.

But I decided I to teach and mentor – to ignite a spark.

I chose to inspire both genders by action and pen.

## Do What's Right

"No, I don't want to be unique."
"The kids will think that I am weak."
"I want to look like my best friend."
"Not be different, simply blend."

My demand was put to bed.
Mom put glasses on my head.
Even worse, an eye patch sat.
I felt as blind as a bat.

"How can I have fun in school?"
I saw scorn and ridicule.
Never did I expect,
Lots of praise and respect.

Reading did not start that year.
But I had the teacher's ear.
I was popular with most.
To others, a whipping post.

Debby Hackbarth

To good counsel I listened.

I prospered and glistened.

Others chose to protest.

Their vision, not the best.


Listen to sound advice.

OR

Your eyes will pay the price.

## Perseverance

I am still a child.

I have so much more to learn, so much more to experience.

I am constantly searching, constantly questioning.

Won't anyone help? Can't anyone help? **NO.**

I must find the world myself, find my mind myself.

I have a long road to travel, a high hill to climb.

I won't give up. I can't give up. **WHY?**

Because if I do, I will cease to exist and will never grow up.


There are always CONFLICTS, RESTRICTIONS, INDECISIVENESS.

So many feeling are present yet FEAR enters in.

FEAR of being hurt, becoming involved, hurting another, ONESELF.

Debby Hackbarth

I have found a new relationship – one primarily
of the mind, FRESH, which my emotions would
like to make STALE.

All need warmth, love, security, protection YET
because of others around them, A **HALT.**

So many warm feelings would like to be
showered, shared.

Once love was sweet – then bitter, shut off.

Will it come again? Will it grow now?

Will I ruin an understanding with love?

Life is a riddle that constantly changes its
answer and makes man question his soul at
every turn.

## **Little Towhead**

Doctors decided to incubate,
No care if eyes couldn't tolerate.
Lungs were fine, but vision injury,
No one foresaw the years of misery.

School days brought pain and ridicule.
Very few showed the golden rule.
Shouts of "4 eyes" sent me crying.
Sheer willpower kept me flying.

Weeks early, I appeared foot-first,
Due to the rules, I was reversed.
Little towhead with crossed eyes.
Didn't know she'd later rise.

How do you mend from maltreatment?
How do you transform from tragedy?
How do you counteract cruelty?

Continue to contemplate outside the norm.

Celebrate life with pride in yourself.

Color outside the lines.

Break out!

## **Spreading Encouragement**

To say we are opposite would be an
understatement.

Born two years apart, we spent our lives
arguing.

A life-long relationship was cursed from
commencement.

Our thoughts about life were constantly
conflicting.


Even our parents viewed our mutual
discontent.

For my part, I sought peace not continuous
clashing.

But she was controlling and liked to torment.

My mission has been to assist others who are
struggling.


As the years passed, I found joy spreading
encouragement.

I mourn for her, but my life is about
harmonizing.

My hope is to leave a legacy of a life well-
spent.

Debby Hackbarth

## Transformation

Encouragement can emanate from anyone.

EXPRESSIONS - GESTURES

Reassurance resounds from loved ones.

PRAISE – EXPECTATIONS

This I will never forget – "best things come in small packages".

TINY, TREMENDOUS

CHILDLIKE, COURAGEOUS

POWERFUL PIONEER

Committed care was a constant companion.

Life was difficult, but driving forward.

ROADBLOCK

TURN IN THE ROAD

FORK IN THE STREAM

This I will never forget – you can't do it.

IDEAS IGNORED

DREAMS DASHED

PLANS PARALYZED.

Realize Reality Resounds with Radiance!

## Chapter Five: Nature

Growing up in a turbulent household, I sought peace in nature. I'd hike with friends for hours, ride my bike for many blocks, and just sit in nearby fields to listen to the birds.

As an adult, I love to be outside. When we lived in the pacific northwest, we discovered places off the main pathways often. Now, living in the south, walks along the bay refresh my soul.

Debby Hackbarth

## Outside

Running outside to play,
And what did I see?

Seven pretty blue jays,
Red butterflies three.

Jumping up to the sky,
Feeling funny and free.

Soon I think I can fly,
Like a yellow bee.

Time to tickle roses,
Swing this way and that.

Black cricket hits my nose,
And I am down – splat.

## Soul Stories

No crying, just sleepy,
So many clouds around.

Very gray and rainy.
To bed, not a sound.

Debby Hackbarth

**Pursuing Peace**


Peace can be found in nature's tranquility.

When the birds are silent and soundless.

All of the flora and fauna abide in harmony.

The forest is overflowing with calmness.

Even overactive insects sense the amity.

Is it too much to ask the humans to be
motionless?


Can mankind actually experience passivity?

I aspire to be stuffed with stillness.

I hope to be soaked with serenity.

For more than one minute, can I be noiseless?

Will I ever be able to experience immobility?

Countryside, cover me with coolness.


Nature teach me equability.

May I finally experience understanding and
quietness.

## Rolling Waves

Fascination forever not far away,
Location often unreachable,
Sounds sweet to the ear.

Childhood journeys,
Teenage escapes,
Artificial settings.

Finally, a chance,
A voyage of many miles,
The trip of a lifetime finally here.

A reunion with an ancient friend.
One special moment to pause,
An occasion to relax, renew.

Walking with anticipation,
Listening, smelling, searching,

Debby Hackbarth

For a glimpse of the rolling waves.

Proximity presents a thunderous roar,

Salty brine like a bumpy blanket,

Aquatic elation throughout.

## The Ocean, A Forever Friend

I rush with expectancy,
Listening, breathless, searching,
To observe the undulating waves.

I experience the thunderous roar.
Salt-water crashes over me like a coverlet.
My entire being pulses with passion.
Dreams fulfilled in a single moment.

My mind has been here often.
I have journeyed here joyously.
Now to be standing in the salty sand.
My soul is satisfied.

Communing with the sea.
The ocean, a forever friend.
I must drink in this moment.
Time to just exist and enjoy.

The soft waves gladden my eyes.
The salty sea has forced a pucker.
The crashing waters hasten peace.
The quests of childhood complete.

Debby Hackbarth

## Searching And Soaring

After the sun falls asleep,
Through a huge telescope I peep.
Ignoring items of the day,
Searching for the Milky Way.

Astounding.

A planet is a ghostly spot,
Flashing in black it can trot.
Not flying on a random trail,
Soaring on a monorail.

Animated.

Life has always been this way,
Interstellar dreams night and day.
Not because of massive tomes,
But from intellectual roams.

Awestruck.

# Soul Stories

One day I will flee the Earth,
Encased in metal, filled with mirth.
Sad to leave family behind,
Proliferating humankind.

Absconding.

Don't morn for me as I go,
This obsession caused me to grow.
Those who know me wish me well,
On other planets I will dwell.

Accomplishment.

Debby Hackbarth

## The Dream

How it must feel,
To reach out and
Touch the black curtain.
To truly see,
The pure beauty
Of the specks of light.

A grand event,
Science flanking,
To be the first one.
Not in a ship, nor in a suit,
A stroke with my palm.

I dream, I wish,
Wait for the day,
When deep space and I,
Walk hand in hand for miles.

## Incorporate Kindness

When nature envelopes you; be aware and
dutiful.

Be considerate of flowering plants and be
watchful.

If you crush them, nectar and pollen won't be
plentiful.

We demonstrate our true nature when we're
thoughtful.

Pay attention to where your feet tread; be
careful.

Animals on the ground could hurt you; be
heedful.

Everyone outside should be sensible and stay
mindful.

If we don't take care of our planet, they'll be
repercussions.

It's time to have serious and intelligent
discussions.

We need to incorporate kindness into our
consciousness.

Debby Hackbarth

## Miss Jane on the Train

For the first time, Jane was traveled
throughout northern Maine.

The distance between villages was too close to
take a plane.

She didn't want to rent a car because the cost
was insane.

Her best choice was to board the attractive
antique train.


Train trips to her grandmother's house were
burned in her brain.

She hoped this trip would be a lovely journey
down memory lane.

The Victorian décor was filled with antiques
from Spain.

The beauty that surrounded her was far from
mundane.


Attentive staff with fantastic food showed no
restrain.

The quaint hamlets on the route filled the
rolling terrain.

# Soul Stories

Each town was more picturesque than the last;
she could not complain.

The jaunts to grandma's place were in a
completely different domain.


On the way home, the clattering old
locomotive gave her a migraine.

The stewards and the nurses tried to help
Jane, in vain.

She spent the final hours of the trip writhing in
pain.

Maybe her next trip on the rails would include
a Pullman train.

Debby Hackbarth

## Chapter Six: Society

"Sadly, we live in a world that's broken.

Folks who hate others are outspoken.

Parents and children are heartbroken.

We need to return to compassion."

The above verses are in one of the following poems. I believe with all of my being that we do need to work together for the betterment of humanity.

We truly do need to "give peace a chance."

Debby Hackbarth

## Return To Compassion

If I had my way, all peoples would live in
peace.

If I had my way, starvation would be out of
reach.

If I had my way, every country would have
free speech.

PERCEPTION, RECOGNITION, APPRECIATION,

Sadly, we live in a world that's broken.

Folks who hate others are outspoken.

Parents and children are heartbroken.

DISPIRITED, DISTURBED, DISAPPOINTED

We need to return to compassion.

The brave must demand a commission.

A courageous and empathetic expedition.

ALTERNESS, RECEPTIVENESS,
REPONSIVENESS

If I had my way, we'd take to the streets
today.

If I had my way, we'd make progress day by
day.

If I had my way, kindness wouldn't be one
way.

GET ON UP, MOVE RIGHT OUT, LEND A HAND

Let's fight prejudice with shared
understanding.

Let's battle bullying by confidence building.

Let's work together loving and forgiving.

CONSIDERATE, SYMPATHETIC,
COMPASSIONATE

No longer can there be hate.

We need our priorities straight.

Relate, advocate, motivate.

IF I HAD MY WAY, PEACE WOULD HAVE A
CHANCE!

Debby Hackbarth

## **Butterflies Into Bliss**

A new mother's life can be filled with fears.

Day and night her concerns could crowd out joy.

BUTTERFLIES

These worries could wear her down with trepidation.

Apprehensions may cancel appreciation.

ANXIETY

Will she be able to care for this new creation?

Can her excitement overcome this uneasiness?

DISCOMFORT

Her support squad can help lessen her stress.

They can help her change tensions into tenderness.

ENCOURAGEMENT

Across the world, there are resources for child rearing.

Advisors can help turn angst into elation.

BLISS

## Failing Fatherhood

Fatherhood has many different definitions.
In most families, it means supervision.

A loving father provides tender care.
In other families, a father is a guardian.

This father is more of a shield of protection.
Unfortunately, some fathers are absent.

These fathers are missing and not around.
They cannot watch over their children

.

Let's come together to help these families.
Let's find ways to support the children.

Debby Hackbarth

## Stand Up For yourself

Our brains are integral parts of us.

They help us to understand the world around us.

Our minds provide common sense as well as reasoning.

PRECIOUS PROVSION

However, there are those who would like to harm us.

Planning our ruin, they will not discuss.

Folks can hurt us without conversing.

BRITTLE BEING

Surrounding yourself with true pals, a plus.

Stand up for yourself, make a fuss.

Plan out each move, constantly contemplating.

DAILY DEFENSE

Use your intellect joyfully, not a "gloomy Gus".

Think of yourself first; no fuss, no muss.

You can still bring joy to others unremitting.

MINDFUL MERCY

## **Enduring Exploration**

There are those who feel exploration involves
only transportation.

However, there are many forms of inquiry that
deserve consideration.


When you are learning a new skill, you may
use visualization.

The visual modality can increase mental
stimulation.


This process can strengthen proficiency
through intensification.

Nevertheless, explorers and travelers held in-
depth investigation.


As they traveled throughout the world gaining
knowledge.

Their journeys brought them to the known-
world edge.


The long voyages were started with a
monetary pledge.

Nonetheless, the ordinary probing person can
acknowledge.

Debby Hackbarth

That all people without previous
foreknowledge.

Are you able to mentally or physically go "out
on a ledge".

Endless, enduring exploration engenders
everlasting elation.

## Living In Unity

We need to care for one another.

The person next to you is your brother.

It's our civic duty to give to others.

Be a support to fathers and mothers.


Until we live in unity, we are never free.

All peoples of the world are from the same
family tree.

Reach out to others in your community.

Show a loving spirit to all in society.


Don't be alone, facilitate fellowship.

With some you'll have a deep friendship.

With others you'll enjoy a warm kinship.

Create a caring companionship.


Form a village in your vicinity.

Pamper people in close proximity.

To help folks you don't need a pedigree.

Let's assist others to love and be free.

Debby Hackbarth

## **Marvelous Multiplicity**

Multiplicity is diversity.

Diversity honors uniqueness.

Uniqueness promotes exceptionality.


Exceptionality merges with extraordinariness.

It's everyone's obligation to value creativity.

As long as expression is done with kindness.


Being connected with others is our
responsibility.

Honoring each other's individuality with
thankfulness.


Our world needs to venerate individuality.

Our leaders must operate with graciousness.

Marvelous multiplicity motivates many to
magnificence.

## Value Others

We were taught to mind or obey our parents.

Did you ever wonder what would happen?

Would you get punished immediately?


It was an absolutely expected that we'd have a talk.

Would a tap on the bum come afterwards?

Could a "grounding" be in our future?


Most of the time we'd have a respectful conversation.

Do all families operate in this fashion?

Should I ask my friends what goes on in their homes?


I decided it was none of my business.

What if someone shared their punishment?

How would I react?

Debby Hackbarth

Unfortunately, one girl showed me her welts.

Should I tell an adult what she revealed to me?

Would respecting her private life be safe for
her?


I decided to do what was best for me for my
life.

Would I grow up to be a responsible adult?

How would I teach my own children respect?


For me, minding my parents taught me to
value others.

Will our grandchildren teach their offspring in
an equivalent manner?

Will our world move toward regarding others
respectfully?

## Parenting: Not An Easy Task

Children thrive in an environment that's honoring.

Parenthood involves persistent principled protection.

GUARDING

Parents can teach values worth sustaining.

Arduous work that's never over and done.

ONGOING

Unfortunately, some families can't provide respectful rearing.

Because of trauma, the home is not well-run.

OPPRESSING

An unhappy mother may become controlling.

A father who is never home is good to no one.

DEPRESSING

However, the family unit is worth preserving.

Reaching for help is always a home run.

DESIRING

Motherhood can cultivate joy and laughing.

Fatherhood can foster happiness for everyone.

GLOWING

Debby Hackbarth

## We Need Redemption

Our world is in a state of deterioration.

All around us, oxidation and corrosion.

Even humans are experiencing degeneration.

There is constant interpersonal conflict and aggravation.

Daily living is filled with chaos, disorder, and confusion.

The planet Earth needs refurbishment and restoration.

What system would be able to provide revitalization?

Someone, please, arrange renovation and reconstruction.

A few compassionate leaders are needed to offer liberation.

Only through cooperation are we able to experience emancipation.

If only the heads of nations are clever enough to grasp this salvation.

Human beings need to swallow their egos and seize this redemption.

## Significant

Do the words I express have importance for others?

I do have faith in mankind and love for all around me.


Remember, you never know the path your life will take.

Life can be challenging but, follow your dreams.


Life is not enjoyed until you find yourself.

Don't let life's challenges stop you.


Perhaps we are only put on earth,

To try and find out where we fit in.


Maybe we are just part of a giant puzzle.

Hopefully, we are significant – each one of us.


No one will ever know.

But we can change the world around us.

Debby Hackbarth

## **Darkness, Disaster, Dream**

We heard the rumbling; we hid in a cave.

DESPERATION

The longer we were there; it felt like a grave.

DEPRESSION

The dreadful noise ceased; we tried to be brave.

ANTICIPATION

The damaged countryside - a terrestrial tidal wave.

REVULSION

The war had surprised everyone; did we misbehave?

CONFUSION

So many had died already; who could we possibly save?

EXPECTATION

## Sparkle In Every Situation

She was born in a lovely garden.
Her mother chose the name Rose.

Immediately, Rose's eyes did glisten.
Her sparkle emanated from head to toes.

Her life was filled with vivaciousness.
She brought humor to every situation.

Every moment was filled with cheerfulness.
No one knew about her condition.

Right after birth, an insect stung her.
The prick left a tiny mark.

She did not cry or make a stir.
As time passed, some saw a birthmark.

Debby Hackbarth

Rose remained joyful and carefree.
However, her growth was arrested.

Doctor after doctor could not agree.
A diagnosis was forever hunted.

Her little body would never mend.
I was afraid I'd lose my best friend.

On the eve of her sixteenth birthday.
Her life ended much to everyone's dismay.

## Unrestrained Rule

Power can be displayed in many ways.

Everyone can calmly communicate the
constructive.


Rather than control, let's stress competence.

A positive approach is more productive.


Instead of delivering defeating domination.

Encouraging expertise is more effective.


Menacing managers can make life miserable.

Join together, plan, and be active


No human requires regulation without respect.

Debby Hackbarth

# **Afterword**

Debby has authored several books and a supplemental reading and writing program for students of all ages. All publications are available from HAART, LLC at dhackbarth7@gmail.com and on her website deborahhackbarth.com:

- The Fairhope Dragon Series
- The Fairhope Dragon Mini Books
- Tee Tree Mini Books – climate focus
- Dynamic Debby: Overcoming Prematurity and Poor Vision – award-winning memoir
- Memory Magic: A Program to Enhance Reading, Writing, and Spelling.

Please check Amazon.com and Barnes and Noble – both the store in AL and online at BN.com for most of these publications.

Debby also offers private tutoring/mentoring sessions, creates commissioned artwork, and is available for motivational speaking engagements at dhackbarth7@gmail.com. Debby's lifelong focus has been to lift up, encourage, and equip others to lead their best lives.

Debby Hackbarth

Visit the Authors Website:

www.DeborahHackbarth.com

www.ingramcontent.com/pod-product-compliance
Lightning Source LLC
Chambersburg PA
CBHW020743130626
46554CB00006B/2116